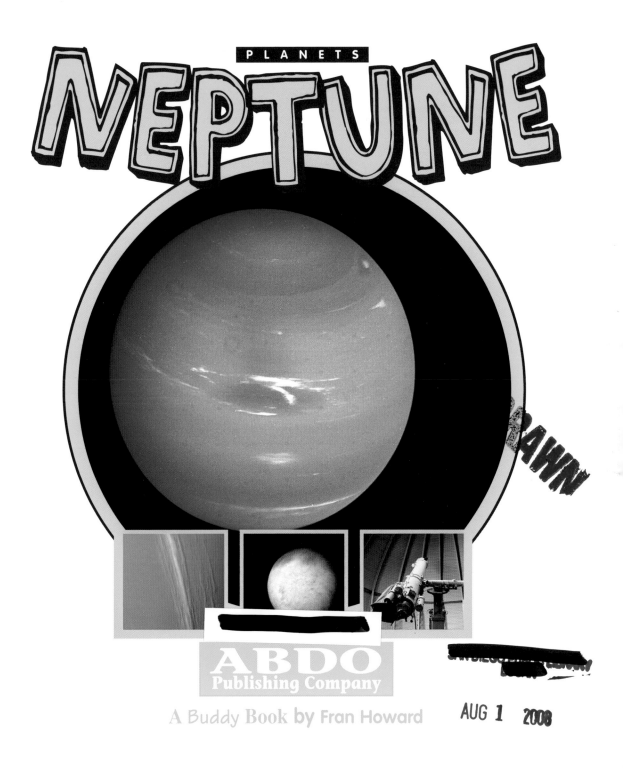

PLANETS

NEPTUNE

ABDO
Publishing Company

A Buddy Book by Fran Howard

VISIT US AT

www.abdopublishing.com

Published by ABDO Publishing Company, 8000 West 78th Street, Edina, Minnesota 55439.

Printed in the United States.

Editor: Sarah Tieck
Contributing Editor: Michael P. Goecke
Graphic Design: Maria Hosley
Cover Image: Lushpix
Interior Images: Library of Congress (page 21); NASA: Goddard Space Flight Center (page 26), Jet Propulsion Laboratory (page 5, 6–7, 9, 11, 12, 13, 17, 25, 28), Space Telescope Science Institute (page 27); Photos.com (page 23).

Library of Congress Cataloging-in-Publication Data

Howard, Fran, 1953-
  Neptune / Fran Howard.
     p. cm. -- (The planets)
  Includes index.
  ISBN 978-1-59928-830-7
  1. Neptune (Planet)--Juvenile literature. I. Title.

  QB691.H69 2008
  523.481--dc22

                                   2007014758

Table Of Contents

The Planet Neptune 4

Our Solar System 6

The Windy Planet 8

A View Of Neptune 10

What Is It Like There? 14

A Gas Giant 18

Discovering Neptune 20

Missions To Neptune 24

Fact Trek 28

Voyage To Tomorrow 30

Important Words 31

Web Sites 31

Index 32

The Planet Neptune

Neptune is a planet. A planet is a large body in space.

Planets travel around stars. The path a planet travels is its orbit. When the planet circles a star, it is orbiting the star.

The sun is a star. Neptune orbits the sun. The sun's **gravity** holds Neptune in place as it circles.

It takes Neptune almost 165 Earth years to orbit the sun. Neptune's orbit is longer than that of any other planet!

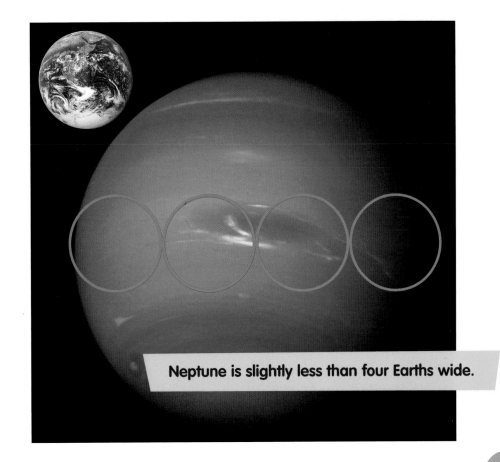

Neptune is slightly less than four Earths wide.

Our Solar System

OUTER PLANETS

Neptune

Uranus

Saturn

Jupiter

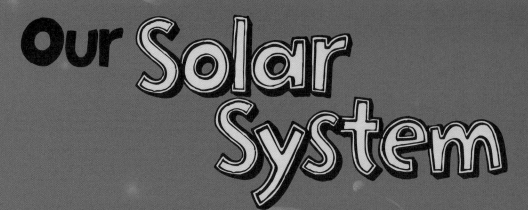

Neptune's Orbit

Neptune is one of eight planets that orbit our sun. The planets orbiting the sun make up our solar system.

The other planets in our solar system are Mercury, Venus, Earth, Mars, Jupiter, Saturn, and Uranus.

Neptune is the farthest planet from the sun. It is almost 3 billion miles (4 billion km) away!

SUN

Mars
Earth
Venus
Mercury

INNER PLANETS

The Windy Planet

Neptune has the strongest winds of any planet. Winds on Neptune often reach 750 miles (1,200 km) per hour. Some even reach 1,200 miles (2,000 km) per hour! Neptune's winds are about seven times stronger than Earth's strongest winds.

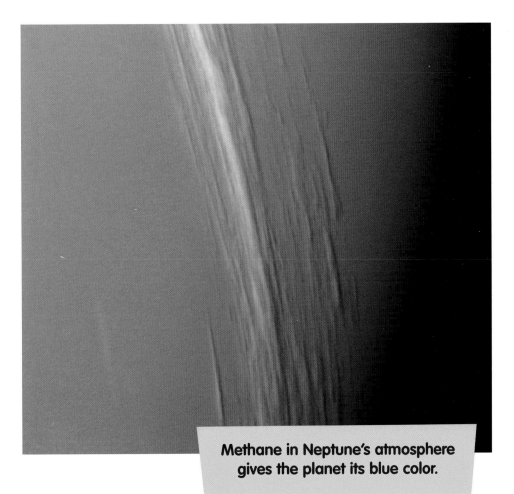

Methane in Neptune's atmosphere gives the planet its blue color.

A View Of Neptune

Neptune is the fourth-largest planet in our solar system. It has five dark-colored rings. Scientists do not know what makes up Neptune's rings. But, they describe the rings as "clumpy."

Scientists say some of Neptune's rings are unstable. They could disappear in less than 100 years.

Neptune's outermost ring is 39,000 miles (63,000 km) away from the planet!

Neptune has 13 known moons. The largest is called Triton.

Triton is an icy moon. It is one of the coldest places in our solar system. Triton even has **geysers** that shoot out ice!

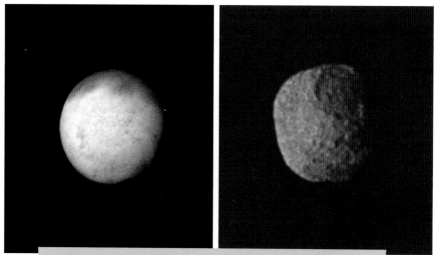

Triton *(left)* was discovered in 1846, just after the discovery of Neptune. The moon 1989N1 *(right)* wasn't discovered until almost 150 years later.

Scientists think Triton may have polar ice caps like Earth.

What Is It Like There?

Layers of gases surround each planet. These layers make up the planet's **atmosphere**. The gases in Neptune's atmosphere include **methane**, hydrogen, and helium.

Planets spin on an **axis**. This spinning creates night and day.

Neptune makes one complete spin in 16 hours and six minutes. So, a day on Neptune is not quite as long as a day on Earth.

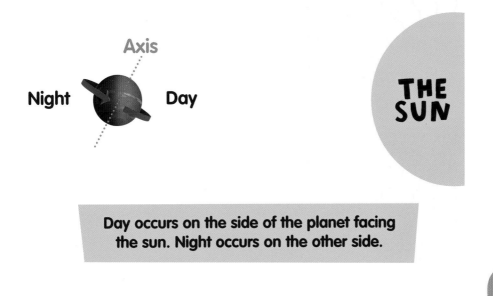

Day occurs on the side of the planet facing the sun. Night occurs on the other side.

For many reasons, scientists do not believe life exists on Neptune.

Neptune is one of the coldest planets in our solar system. It has ice in its core and atmosphere. Sometimes this planet is called an ice giant.

Neptune's middle layer, or mantle, is hotter than the sun's surface! These extreme temperatures cause violent weather. So, the planet has many large storms.

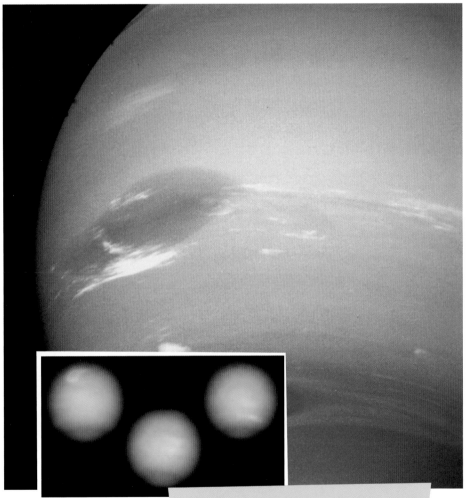

Neptune's appearance changes
as clouds and storms move.

A Gas Giant

Neptune does not have a surface to stand on. This is because it is a gas giant. Gas giants are mostly made of gas. Saturn, Uranus, and Jupiter are also gas giants.

Though there's no surface, Neptune's hot mantle is filled with water, ammonia, and methane.

Scientists say Neptune contains solid matter that is about the size of Earth! This is Neptune's core.

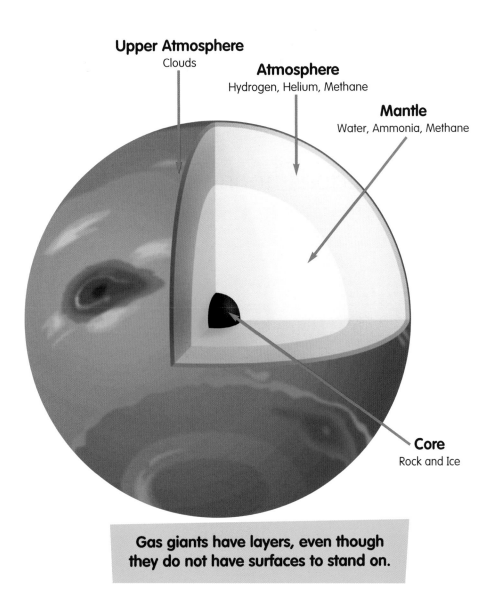

Upper Atmosphere
Clouds

Atmosphere
Hydrogen, Helium, Methane

Mantle
Water, Ammonia, Methane

Core
Rock and Ice

Gas giants have layers, even though they do not have surfaces to stand on.

Discovering Neptune

When Galileo first saw Neptune in 1612, he thought it was a star. So, this planet wasn't officially discovered until September 23, 1846.

Neptune is the first planet to be discovered using mathematics. While studying Uranus, scientists noticed its unusual orbit. They believed this meant there was another object beyond Uranus. Scientists used mathematics to guess where this object should be. It was right where they thought!

Galileo was an Italian astronomer. He made simple telescopes to help him study the sky.

English astronomer and mathematician John C. Adams *(left)* and French mathematician Urbain J.J. Leverrier *(right)* used mathematics to find Neptune's position.

Soon, 165 years will have passed since Neptune was discovered. At that time, the planet will return to the exact spot it was when scientists discovered it.

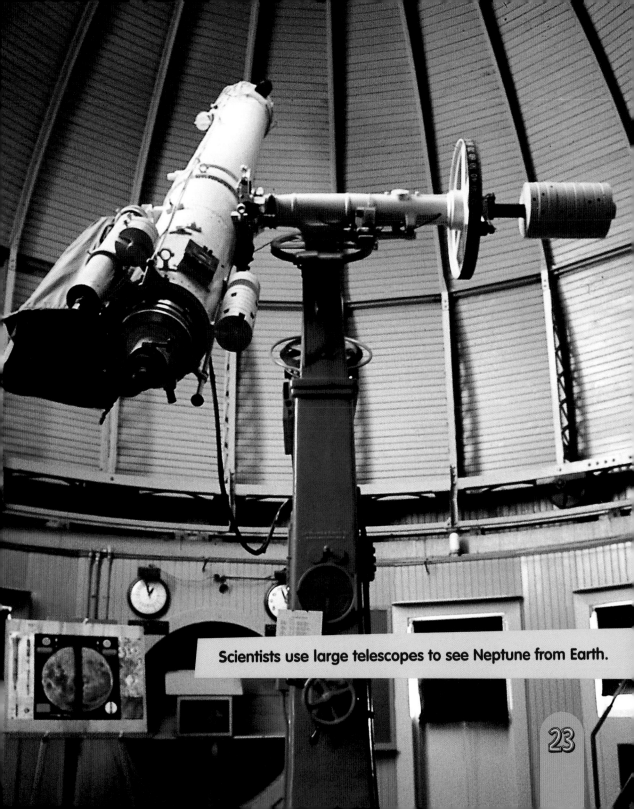

Scientists use large telescopes to see Neptune from Earth.

23

Missions To Neptune

The *Voyager 2* **probe** is the only **spacecraft** to visit Neptune. That was in August 1989.

Voyager 2 discovered that Neptune had a Great Dark Spot. It was a storm the size of Earth.

Voyager 2 also discovered Neptune's strong winds. These winds surprised scientists. They did not expect Neptune to have stronger winds than Jupiter!

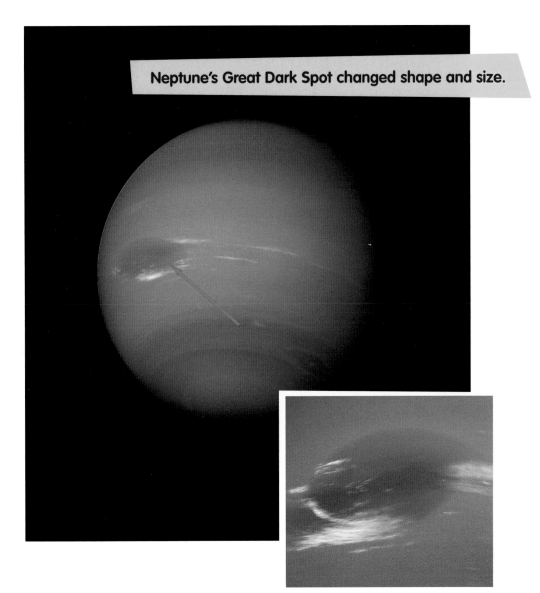

Neptune's Great Dark Spot changed shape and size.

The Hubble Space Telescope **orbits** Earth. It has shown more recent activity on Neptune. Scientists say the Great Dark Spot has disappeared. But other storms have formed.

Hubble discovered a new dark spot on northern Neptune.

The Hubble Space Telescope provides scientists with information about the planets and distant stars. It will orbit Earth until 2013.

From Earth, you need a telescope to see Neptune. It looks like a small, blue-green disk.

About 60 Earths could fit inside Neptune!

Neptune is named after the Roman god of the sea. Its symbol is a three-pronged spear. It represents the spear that Neptune used to control the oceans and the seas.

Voyage To Tomorrow

People are continuing to explore space. They want to learn more about Neptune.

NASA is planning another **mission** to Neptune. This mission is called the *Neptune/Triton Orbiter*. It will launch in 2035. Scientists hope they will learn more about Neptune's rings and moons.

Important Words

atmosphere   the layer of gases that surrounds a planet.

axis   an imaginary line through a planet. Planets spin around this line.

geyser   a spring that shoots out hot water and steam.

gravity   the force that draws things toward a planet and prevents them from floating away. Stars use this force to keep planets in their orbit.

methane   an odorless, colorless gas that burns easily. Sometimes it is used for fuel.

mission   the sending of spacecraft to perform specific jobs.

NASA   National Aeronautics and Space Administration.

probe   a spacecraft that attempts to gather information.

spacecraft   a vehicle that travels in space.

Web Sites

To learn more about **Neptune**, visit ABDO Publishing Company on the World Wide Web. Web sites about **Neptune** are featured on our Book Links page. These links are routinely monitored and updated to provide the most current information available.

www.abdopublishing.com

INDEX

Adams, John C. **22**

atmosphere **9, 14, 19**

axis **15**

core **18, 19**

Earth **5, 7, 8, 13, 15, 18, 23, 24, 26, 27, 28**

Galileo **20, 21**

gases **9, 14, 18, 19**

gravity **4**

Great Dark Spot **24, 25, 26**

Hubble Space Telescope **26, 27**

ice **12, 13, 16, 19**

Jupiter **6, 7, 18, 24**

Leverrier, Urbain J.J. **22**

mantle **16, 18, 19**

Mars **7**

Mercury **7**

missions **24, 30**

moons (Neptune) **12, 13, 30**

NASA **30**

orbit **4, 5, 6, 30**

rings **10, 11, 30**

Romans **29**

Saturn **6, 7, 18**

solar system **6, 7, 10, 12, 16**

storms **16, 17, 26**

sun **4, 5, 6, 7, 15, 16**

telescope **21, 23, 26, 27, 28**

Uranus **6, 7, 18, 20**

Venus **7**

winds **8, 24**